'Woman much missed, how you call to me, call to me . . .'

THOMAS HARDY

Born 1840, Higher Bockhampton, near Dorchester, England
Died 1928, Dorchester, England

In 1870, Thomas Hardy went to Cornwall, where he met and fell in love with Emma Gifford, his first wife. Emma's death, on 27 November 1912, inspired some of the finest verse of Hardy's career, including the sequence 'Poems 1912–13'. This selection includes these poems, along with others relating to Hardy's courtship, marriage and widowed life.

# THOMAS HARDY

## *Woman much missed*

PENGUIN BOOKS

PENGUIN CLASSICS

Published by the Penguin Group
Penguin Books Ltd, 80 Strand, London WC2R ORL, England
Penguin Group (USA) Inc., 375 Hudson Street, New York, New York 10014, USA
Penguin Group (Canada), 90 Eglinton Avenue East, Suite 700, Toronto, Ontario,
Canada M4P 2Y3 (a division of Pearson Penguin Canada Inc.)
Penguin Ireland, 25 St Stephen's Green, Dublin 2, Ireland
(a division of Penguin Books Ltd)
Penguin Group (Australia), 707 Collins Street, Melbourne, Victoria 3008, Australia
(a division of Pearson Australia Group Pty Ltd)
Penguin Books India Pvt Ltd, 11 Community Centre, Panchsheel Park,
New Delhi – 110 017, India
Penguin Group (NZ), 67 Apollo Drive, Rosedale, Auckland 0632, New Zealand
(a division of Pearson New Zealand Ltd)
Penguin Books (South Africa) (Pty) Ltd, Block D, Rosebank Office Park,
181 Jan Smuts Avenue, Parktown North, Gauteng 2193, South Africa

Penguin Books Ltd, Registered Offices: 80 Strand, London WC2R ORL, England

www.penguin.com

This selection published in Penguin Classics 2015
001

Set in 9.5/13 pt Baskerville 10 Pro
Typeset by Jouve (UK), Milton Keynes
Printed in Great Britain by Clays Ltd, St Ives plc

A CIP catalogue record for this book is available from the British Library

ISBN: 978-0-141-39831-0

www.greenpenguin.co.uk

Penguin Books is committed to a sustainable
future for our business, our readers and our planet.
This book is made from Forest Stewardship
Council™ certified paper.

# Contents

## 'When I Set Out for Lyonnesse'

### 1870

When I set out for Lyonnesse,
  A hundred miles away,
  The rime was on the spray,
And starlight lit my lonesomeness
When I set out for Lyonnesse
  A hundred miles away.

What would bechance at Lyonnesse
  While I should sojourn there
  No prophet durst declare,
Nor did the wisest wizard guess
What would bechance at Lyonnesse
  While I should sojourn there.

When I came back from Lyonnesse
  With magic in my eyes,
  All marked with mute surmise
My radiance rare and fathomless,
When I came back from Lyonnesse
  With magic in my eyes!

## Shut Out That Moon

Close up the casement, draw the blind,
    Shut out that stealing moon,
She wears too much the guise she wore
    Before our lutes were strewn
With years-deep dust, and names we read
    On a white stone were hewn.

Step not forth on the dew-dashed lawn
    To view the Lady's Chair,
Immense Orion's glittering form,
    The Less and Greater Bear:
Stay in; to such sights we were drawn
    When faded ones were fair.

Brush not the bough for midnight scents
    That come forth lingeringly,
And wake the same sweet sentiments
    They breathed to you and me
When living seemed a laugh, and love
    All it was said to be.

Within the common lamp-lit room
  Prison my eyes and thought;
Let dingy details crudely loom,
  Mechanic speech be wrought:
Too fragrant was Life's early bloom,
  Too tart the fruit it brought!

POEMS OF 1912—13

*Veteris vestigia flammae*

## The Going

Why did you give no hint that night
That quickly after the morrow's dawn,
And calmly, as if indifferent quite,
You would close your term here, up and be gone
      Where I could not follow
      With wing of swallow
To gain one glimpse of you ever anon!

      Never to bid good-bye,
      Or lip me the softest call,
Or utter a wish for a word, while I
Saw morning harden upon the wall,
      Unmoved, unknowing
      That your great going
Had place that moment, and altered all.

Why do you make me leave the house
And think for a breath it is you I see
At the end of the alley of bending boughs

Where so often at dusk you used to be;
      Till in darkening dankness
      The yawning blankness
Of the perspective sickens me!

      You were she who abode
      By those red-veined rocks far West,
You were the swan-necked one who rode
Along the beetling Beeny Crest,
      And, reining nigh me,
      Would muse and eye me,
While Life unrolled us its very best.

Why, then, latterly did we not speak,
Did we not think of those days long dead,
And ere your vanishing strive to seek
That time's renewal? We might have said,
      'In this bright spring weather
      We'll visit together
Those places that once we visited.'

      Well, well! All's past amend,
      Unchangeable. It must go.
I seem but a dead man held on end
To sink down soon . . . O you could not know
      That such swift fleeing
      No soul foreseeing –
Not even I – would undo me so!

## Your Last Drive

Here by the moorway you returned,
And saw the borough lights ahead
That lit your face – all undiscerned
To be in a week the face of the dead,
And you told of the charm of that haloed view
That never again would beam on you.

And on your left you passed the spot
Where eight days later you were to lie,
And be spoken of as one who was not;
Beholding it with a heedless eye
As alien from you, though under its tree
You soon would halt everlastingly.

I drove not with you . . . Yet had I sat
At your side that eve I should not have seen
That the countenance I was glancing at
Had a last-time look in the flickering sheen,
Nor have read the writing upon your face,
'I go hence soon to my resting-place;

'You may miss me then. But I shall not know
How many times you visit me there,
Or what your thoughts are, or if you go
There never at all. And I shall not care.

Should you censure me I shall take no heed,
And even your praises no more shall need.'

True: never you'll know. And you will not mind.
But shall I then slight you because of such?
Dear ghost, in the past did you ever find
The thought 'What profit,' move me much?
Yet abides the fact, indeed, the same, –
You are past love, praise, indifference, blame.

## The Walk

You did not walk with me
Of late to the hill-top tree
    By the gated ways,
    As in earlier days;
    You were weak and lame,
    So you never came,
And I went alone, and I did not mind,
Not thinking of you as left behind.

I walked up there to-day
Just in the former way;
    Surveyed around
    The familiar ground
    By myself again:
    What difference, then?
Only that underlying sense
Of the look of a room on returning thence.

## Rain on a Grave

Clouds spout upon her
    Their waters amain
    In ruthless disdain, –
Her who but lately
    Had shivered with pain
As at touch of dishonour
If there had lit on her
So coldly, so straightly
    Such arrows of rain:

One who to shelter
    Her delicate head
Would quicken and quicken
    Each tentative tread
If drops chanced to pelt her
    That summertime spills
    In dust-paven rills
When thunder-clouds thicken
    And birds close their bills.

Would that I lay there
    And she were housed here!
Or better, together
Were folded away there
Exposed to one weather
We both, – who would stray there

When sunny the day there,
    Or evening was clear
    At the prime of the year.

Soon will be growing
    Green blades from her mound,
And daisies be showing
    Like stars on the ground,
Till she form part of them –
Ay – the sweet heart of them,
Loved beyond measure
With a child's pleasure
    All her life's round.

## 'I Found Her Out There'

I found her out there
On a slope few see,
That falls westwardly
To the salt-edged air,
Where the ocean breaks
On the purple strand,
And the hurricane shakes
The solid land.

I brought her here,
And have laid her to rest
In a noiseless nest
No sea beats near.
She will never be stirred
In her loamy cell
By the waves long heard
And loved so well.

So she does not sleep
By those haunted heights
The Atlantic smites
And the blind gales sweep,
Whence she often would gaze
At Dundagel's famed head,
While the dipping blaze
Dyed her face fire-red;

And would sigh at the tale
Of sunk Lyonnesse,
As a wind-tugged tress
Flapped her cheek like a flail;
Or listen at whiles
With a thought-bound brow
To the murmuring miles
She is far from now.

Yet her shade, maybe,
Will creep underground
Till it catch the sound
Of that western sea
As it swells and sobs
Where she once domiciled,
And joy in its throbs
With the heart of a child.

## *Without Ceremony*

It was your way, my dear,
To vanish without a word
When callers, friends, or kin
Had left, and I hastened in
To rejoin you, as I inferred.

And when you'd a mind to career
Off anywhere – say to town –
You were all on a sudden gone
Before I had thought thereon,
Or noticed your trunks were down.

So, now that you disappear
For ever in that swift style,
Your meaning seems to me
Just as it used to be:
'Good-bye is not worth while!'

## *Lament*

How she would have loved
A party to-day! –
Bright-hatted and gloved,
With table and tray
And chairs on the lawn
Her smiles would have shone
With welcomings . . . But
She is shut, she is shut
    From friendship's spell
    In the jailing shell
    Of her tiny cell.

Or she would have reigned
At a dinner to-night
With ardours unfeigned,
And a generous delight:
All in her abode
She'd have freely bestowed
On her guests . . . But alas,
She is shut under grass
    Where no cups flow,
    Powerless to know
    That it might be so.

And she would have sought
With a child's eager glance

The shy snowdrops brought
By the new year's advance,
And peered in the rime
Of Candlemas-time
For crocuses . . . chanced
It that she were not tranced
    From sights she loved best;
    Wholly possessed
    By an infinite rest!

And we are here staying
Amid these stale things,
Who care not for gaying,
And those junketings
That used so to joy her,
And never to cloy her
As us they cloy! . . . But
She is shut, she is shut
    From the cheer of them, dead
    To all done and said
    In her yew-arched bed.

## The Haunter

He does not think that I haunt here nightly:
    How shall I let him know
That whither his fancy sets him wandering
    I, too, alertly go? –
Hover and hover a few feet from him
    Just as I used to do,
But cannot answer the words he lifts me –
    Only listen thereto!

When I could answer he did not say them:
    When I could let him know
How I would like to join in his journeys
    Seldom he wished to go.
Now that he goes and wants me with him
    More than he used to do,
Never he sees my faithful phantom
    Though he speaks thereto.

Yes, I companion him to places
    Only dreamers know,
Where the shy hares print long paces,
    Where the night rooks go;
Into old aisles where the past is all to him,
    Close as his shade can do,
Always lacking the power to call to him,
    Near as I reach thereto!

What a good haunter I am, O tell him!
        Quickly make him know
If he but sigh since my loss befell him
        Straight to his side I go.
Tell him a faithful one is doing
        All that love can do
Still that his path may be worth pursuing,
        And to bring peace thereto.

## The Voice

Woman much missed, how you call to me, call to me,
Saying that now you are not as you were
When you had changed from the one who was all to me,
But as at first, when our day was fair.

Can it be you that I hear? Let me view you, then,
Standing as when I drew near to the town
Where you would wait for me: yes, as I knew you then,
Even to the original air-blue gown!

Or is it only the breeze, in its listlessness
Travelling across the wet mead to me here,
You being ever dissolved to wan wistlessness,
Heard no more again far or near?

    Thus I; faltering forward,
    Leaves around me falling,
Wind oozing thin through the thorn from norward,
    And the woman calling.

## His Visitor

I come across from Mellstock while the moon wastes
                          weaker
To behold where I lived with you for twenty years and
                          more:
I shall go in the gray, at the passing of the mail-train,
And need no setting open of the long familiar door
                          As before.

The change I notice in my once own quarters!
A formal-fashioned border where the daisies used to be,
The rooms new painted, and the pictures altered,
And other cups and saucers, and no cosy nook for tea
                          As with me.

I discern the dim faces of the sleep-wrapt servants;
They are not those who tended me through feeble hours
                          and strong,
But strangers quite, who never knew my rule here,
Who never saw me painting, never heard my softling song
                          Float along.

So I don't want to linger in this re-decked dwelling,
I feel too uneasy at the contrasts I behold,
And I make again for Mellstock to return here never,
And rejoin the roomy silence, and the mute and manifold
                          Souls of old.

## A Circular

As 'legal representative'
I read a missive not my own,
On new designs the senders give
    For clothes, in tints as shown.

Here figure blouses, gowns for tea,
And presentation-trains of state,
Charming ball-dresses, millinery,
    Warranted up to date.

And this gay-pictured, spring-time shout
Of Fashion, hails what lady proud?
Her who before last year ebbed out
    Was costumed in a shroud.

## A Dream or No

Why go to Saint-Juliot? What's Juliot to me?
    Some strange necromancy
    But charmed me to fancy
That much of my life claims the spot as its key.

Yes. I have had dreams of that place in the West,
    And a maiden abiding
    Thereat as in hiding;
Fair-eyed and white-shouldered, broad-browed and
        brown-tressed.

And of how, coastward bound on a night long ago,
    There lonely I found her,
    The sea-birds around her,
And other than nigh things uncaring to know.

So sweet her life there (in my thought has it seemed)
    That quickly she drew me
    To take her unto me,
And lodge her long years with me. Such have I
        dreamed.

But nought of that maid from Saint-Juliot I see;
    Can she ever have been here,
    And shed her life's sheen here,
The woman I thought a long housemate with me?

Does there even a place like Saint-Juliot exist?
    Or a Vallency Valley
    With stream and leafed alley,
Or Beeny, or Bos with its flounce flinging mist?

## *After a Journey*

Hereto I come to view a voiceless ghost;
   Whither, O whither will its whim now draw me?
Up the cliff, down, till I'm lonely, lost,
   And the unseen waters' ejaculations awe me.
Where you will next be there's no knowing,
      Facing round about me everywhere,
            With your nut-coloured hair,
And gray eyes, and rose-flush coming and going.

Yes: I have re-entered your olden haunts at last;
   Through the years, through the dead scenes I have
         tracked you;
What have you now found to say of our past –
   Scanned across the dark space wherein I have lacked
      you?
Summer gave us sweets, but autumn wrought division?
   Things were not lastly as firstly well
         With us twain, you tell?
But all's closed now, despite Time's derision.

I see what you are doing: you are leading me on
   To the spots we knew when we haunted here
         together,
The waterfall, above which the mist-bow shone
   At the then fair hour in the then fair weather,

And the cave just under, with a voice still so hollow
    That it seems to call out to me from forty years ago,
        When you were all aglow,
And not the thin ghost that I now frailly follow!

Ignorant of what there is flitting here to see,
    The waked birds preen and the seals flop lazily,
Soon you will have, Dear, to vanish from me,
    For the stars close their shutters and the dawn
        whitens hazily.
Trust me, I mind not, though Life lours,
    The bringing me here; nay, bring me here again!
        I am just the same as when
Our days were a joy, and our paths through flowers.

PENTARGAN BAY

## A Death-Day Recalled

Beeny did not quiver,
  Juliot grew not gray,
Thin Valency's river
  Held its wonted way.
Bos seemed not to utter
  Dimmest note of dirge,
Targan mouth a mutter
  To its creamy surge.

Yet though these, unheeding,
  Listless, passed the hour
Of her spirit's speeding,
  She had, in her flower,
Sought and loved the places –
  Much and often pined
For their lonely faces
  When in towns confined.

Why did not Valency
  In his purl deplore
One whose haunts were whence he
  Drew his limpid store?
Why did Bos not thunder,
  Targan apprehend
Body and Breath were sunder
  Of their former friend?

# *Beeny Cliff*

## (March 1870–March 1913)

### I

O the opal and the sapphire of that wandering western
    sea,
And the woman riding high above with bright hair
    flapping free –
The woman whom I loved so, and who loyally loved me.

### II

The pale mews plained below us, and the waves seemed
    far away
In a nether sky, engrossed in saying their ceaseless
    babbling say,
As we laughed light-heartedly aloft on that clear-sunned
    March day.

### III

A little cloud then cloaked us, and there flew an irised
    rain,
And the Atlantic dyed its levels with a dull misfeatured
    stain,
And then the sun burst out again, and purples prinked
    the main.

## IV

– Still in all its chasmal beauty bulks old Beeny to the
    sky,
And shall she and I not go there once again now March
    is nigh,
And the sweet things said in that March say anew there
    by and by?

## V

What if still in chasmal beauty looms that wild weird
    western shore,
The woman now is – elsewhere – whom the ambling
    pony bore,
And nor knows nor cares for Beeny, and will laugh there
    nevermore.

## At Castle Boterel

As I drive to the junction of lane and highway,
   And the drizzle bedrenches the waggonette,
I look behind at the fading byway,
   And see on its slope, now glistening wet,
      Distinctly yet

Myself and a girlish form benighted
   In dry March weather. We climb the road
Beside a chaise. We had just alighted
   To ease the sturdy pony's load
      When he sighed and slowed.

What we did as we climbed, and what we talked of
   Matters not much, nor to what it led, –
Something that life will not be balked of
   Without rude reason till hope is dead,
      And feeling fled.

It filled but a minute. But was there ever
   A time of such quality, since or before,
In that hill's story? To one mind never,
   Though it has been climbed, foot-swift, foot-sore,
      By thousands more.

Primaeval rocks form the road's steep border,
 And much have they faced there, first and last,
Of the transitory in Earth's long order;
 But what they record in colour and cast
  Is – that we two passed.

And to me, though Time's unflinching rigour,
 In mindless rote, has ruled from sight
The substance now, one phantom figure
 Remains on the slope, as when that night
  Saw us alight.

I look and see it there, shrinking, shrinking,
 I look back at it amid the rain
For the very last time; for my sand is sinking,
 And I shall traverse old love's domain
  Never again.

## Places

Nobody says: Ah, that is the place
Where chanced, in the hollow of years ago,
What none of the Three Towns cared to know –
The birth of a little girl of grace –
The sweetest the house saw, first or last;
        Yet it was so
        On that day long past.

Nobody thinks: There, there she lay
In a room by the Hoe, like the bud of a flower,
And listened, just after the bedtime hour,
To the stammering chimes that used to play
The quaint Old Hundred-and-Thirteenth tune
        In Saint Andrew's tower
        Night, morn, and noon.

Nobody calls to mind that here
Upon Boterel Hill, where the waggoners skid,
With cheeks whose airy flush outbid
Fresh fruit in bloom, and free of fear,
She cantered down, as if she must fall
        (Though she never did),
        To the charm of all.

Nay: one there is to whom these things,
That nobody else's mind calls back,

Have a savour that scenes in being lack,
And a presence more than the actual brings;
To whom to-day is beneaped and stale,
        And its urgent clack
        But a vapid tale.

## The Phantom Horsewoman

Queer are the ways of a man I know:
        He comes and stands
        In a careworn craze,
        And looks at the sands
        And the seaward haze
        With moveless hands
        And face and gaze,
        Then turns to go . . .
And what does he see when he gazes so?

II

They say he sees as an instant thing
        More clear than to-day,
        A sweet soft scene
        That once was in play
        By that briny green;
        Yes, notes alway
        Warm, real, and keen,
        What his back years bring –
A phantom of his own figuring.

Of this vision of his they might say more:
   Not only there
   Does he see this sight,
  But everywhere
  In his brain – day, night,
  As if on the air
  It were drawn rose bright –
  Yea, far from that shore
Does he carry this vision of heretofore:

A ghost-girl-rider. And though, toil-tried,
   He withers daily,
   Time touches her not,
  But she still rides gaily
  In his rapt thought
  On that shagged and shaly
  Atlantic spot,
  And as when first eyed
Draws rein and sings to the swing of the tide.

## The Spell of the Rose

'I mean to build a hall anon,
    And shape two turrets there,
    And a broad newelled stair,
And a cool well for crystal water;
    Yes; I will build a hall anon,
    Plant roses love shall feed upon,
    And apple-trees and pear.'

He set to build the manor-hall,
    And shaped the turrets there,
    And the broad newelled stair,
And the cool well for crystal water;
    He built for me that manor-hall,
    And planted many trees withal,
    But no rose anywhere.

And as he planted never a rose
    That bears the flower of love,
    Though other flowers throve
Some heart-bane moved our souls to sever
    Since he had planted never a rose;
    And misconceits raised horrid shows,
    And agonies came thereof.

'I'll mend these miseries,' then said I,
    And so, at dead of night,
    I went and, screened from sight,
That nought should keep our souls in severance,
    I set a rose-bush. 'This,' said I,
    'May end divisions dire and wry,
    And long-drawn days of blight.'

But I was called from earth – yea, called
    Before my rose-bush grew;
    And would that now I knew
What feels he of the tree I planted,
    And whether, after I was called
    To be a ghost, he, as of old,
    Gave me his heart anew!

Perhaps now blooms that queen of trees
    I set but saw not grow,
    And he, beside its glow –
Eyes couched of the mis-vision that blurred me –
    Ay, there beside that queen of trees
    He sees me as I was, though sees
    Too late to tell me so!

## St Launce's Revisited

Slip back, Time!
Yet again I am nearing
Castle and keep, uprearing
Gray, as in my prime.

At the inn
Smiling nigh, why is it
Not as on my visit
When hope and I were twin?

Groom and jade
Whom I found here, moulder;
Strange the tavern-holder,
Strange the tap-maid.

Here I hired
Horse and man for bearing
Me on my wayfaring
To the door desired.

Evening gloomed
As I journeyed forward
To the faces shoreward,
Till their dwelling loomed.

If again
Towards the Atlantic sea there
I should speed, they'd be there
Surely now as then? . . .

Why waste thought,
When I know them vanished
Under earth; yea, banished
Ever into nought!

## *Where the Picnic Was*

Where we made the fire
In the summer time
Of branch and briar
On the hill to the sea,
I slowly climb
Through winter mire,
And scan and trace
The forsaken place
Quite readily.

Now a cold wind blows,
And the grass is gray,
But the spot still shows
As a burnt circle – aye,
And stick-ends, charred,
Still strew the sward
Whereon I stand,
Last relic of the band
Who came that day!

Yes, I am here
Just as last year,
And the sea breathes brine
From its strange straight line
Up hither, the same
As when we four came.

– But two have wandered far
From this grassy rise
Into urban roar
Where no picnics are,
And one – has shut her eyes
For evermore.

# 'We Sat at the Window'

## (*Bournemouth, 1875*)

We sat at the window looking out,
And the rain came down like silken strings
That Swithin's day. Each gutter and spout
Babbled unchecked in the busy way
    Of witless things:
Nothing to read, nothing to see
Seemed in that room for her and me
    On Swithin's day.

We were irked by the scene, by our own selves; yes,
For I did not know, nor did she infer
How much there was to read and guess
By her in me, and to see and crown
    By me in her.
Wasted were two souls in their prime,
And great was the waste, that July time
    When the rain came down.

## At the Word 'Farewell'

She looked like a bird from a cloud
    On the clammy lawn,
Moving alone, bare-browed
    In the dim of dawn.
The candles alight in the room
    For my parting meal
Made all things withoutdoors loom
    Strange, ghostly, unreal.

The hour itself was a ghost,
    And it seemed to me then
As of chances the chance furthermost
    I should see her again.
I beheld not where all was so fleet
    That a Plan of the past
Which had ruled us from birthtime to meet
    Was in working at last:

No prelude did I there perceive
    To a drama at all,
Or foreshadow what fortune might weave
    From beginnings so small;
But I rose as if quicked by a spur
    I was bound to obey,
And stepped through the casement to her
    Still alone in the gray.

'I am leaving you . . . Farewell!' I said
    As I followed her on
By an alley bare boughs overspread;
    'I soon must be gone!'
Even then the scale might have been turned
    Against love by a feather,
– But crimson one cheek of hers burned
    When we came in together.

## Once at Swanage

The spray sprang up across the cusps of the moon,
    And all its light loomed green
    As a witch-flame's weirdsome sheen
At the minute of an incantation scene;
And it greened our gaze – that night at demilune.

Roaring high and roaring low was the sea
    Behind the headland shores:
    It symboled the slamming of doors,
Or a regiment hurrying over hollow floors . . .
And there we two stood, hands clasped; I and she!

## The Musical Box

Lifelong to be
Seemed the fair colour of the time;
That there was standing shadowed near
A spirit who sang to the gentle chime
Of the self-struck notes, I did not hear,
     I did not see.

Thus did it sing
To the mindless lyre that played indoors
As she came to listen for me without:
'O value what the nonce outpours –
This best of life – that shines about
     Your welcoming!'

I had slowed along
After the torrid hours were done,
Though still the posts and walls and road
Flung back their sense of the hot-faced sun,
And had walked by Stourside Mill, where broad
     Stream-lilies throng.

And I descried
 The dusky house that stood apart,
 And her, white-muslined, waiting there
In the porch with high-expectant heart,
While still the thin mechanic air
        Went on inside.

        At whiles would flit
Swart bats, whose wings, be-webbed and tanned,
Whirred like the wheels of ancient clocks:
She laughed a hailing as she scanned
Me in the gloom, the tuneful box
        Intoning it.

        Lifelong to be
I thought it. That there watched hard by
A spirit who sang to the indoor tune,
'O make the most of what is nigh!'
I did not hear in my dull soul-swoon –
        I did not see.

## A Second Attempt

Thirty years after
I began again
An old-time passion:
And it seemed as fresh as when
The first day ventured on:
When mutely I would waft her
In Love's past fashion
Dreams much dwelt upon,
Dreams I wished she knew.

I went the course through,
From Love's fresh-found sensation –
Remembered still so well –
To worn words charged anew,
That left no more to tell:
Thence to hot hopes and fears,
And thence to consummation,
And thence to sober years,
Markless, and mellow-hued.

Firm the whole fabric stood,
Or seemed to stand, and sound
As it had stood before.
But nothing backward climbs,
And when I looked around

As at the former times,
There was Life – pale and hoar;
And slow it said to me,
'Twice-over cannot be!'

## He Prefers Her Earthly

This after-sunset is a sight for seeing,
Cliff-heads of craggy cloud surrounding it.
　　– And dwell you in that glory-show?
You may; for there are strange strange things in being,
　　　Stranger than I know.

Yet if that chasm of splendour claim your presence
Which glows between the ash cloud and the dun,
　　How changed must be your mortal mould!
Changed to a firmament-riding earthless essence
　　　From what you were of old:

All too unlike the fond and fragile creature
Then known to me . . . Well, shall I say it plain?
　　I would not have you thus and there,
But still would grieve on, missing you, still feature
　　　You as the one you were.

## The Shadow on the Stone

I went by the Druid stone
    That broods in the garden white and lone,
And I stopped and looked at the shifting shadows
    That at some moments fall thereon
    From the tree hard by with a rhythmic swing,
    And they shaped in my imagining
To the shade that a well-known head and shoulders
    Threw there when she was gardening.

I thought her behind my back,
    Yea, her I long had learned to lack,
And I said: 'I am sure you are standing behind me,
    Though how do you get into this old track?'
    And there was no sound but the fall of a leaf
    As a sad response; and to keep down grief
I would not turn my head to discover
    That there was nothing in my belief.

Yet I wanted to look and see
    That nobody stood at the back of me;
But I thought once more: 'Nay, I'll not unvision
    A shape which, somehow, there may be.'
    So I went on softly from the glade,
    And left her behind me throwing her shade,
As she were indeed an apparition –
    My head unturned lest my dream should fade.

## 'She Did Not Turn'

She did not turn,
But passed foot-faint with averted head
In her gown of green, by the bobbing fern,
Though I leaned over the gate that led
From where we waited with table spread;
    But she did not turn:
Why was she near there if love had fled?

    She did not turn,
Though the gate was whence I had often sped
In the mists of morning to meet her, and learn
Her heart, when its moving moods I read
As a book – she mine, as she sometimes said;
    But she did not turn,
And passed foot-faint with averted head.

## A Two-Years' Idyll

Yes; such it was;
Just those two seasons unsought,
Sweeping like summertide wind on our ways;
Moving, as straws,
Hearts quick as ours in those days;
Going like wind, too, and rated as nought
Save as the prelude to plays
Soon to come – larger, life-fraught:
Yes; such it was.

'Nought' it was called,
Even by ourselves – that which springs
Out of the years for all flesh, first or last,
Commonplace, scrawled
Dully on days that go past.
Yet, all the while, it upbore us like wings
Even in hours overcast:
Aye, though this best thing of things,
'Nought' it was called!

What seems it now?
Lost: such beginning was all;
Nothing came after: romance straight forsook
Quickly somehow
Life when we sped from our nook,

Primed for new scenes with designs smart and tall . . .
    – A preface without any book,
  A trumpet uplipped, but no call;
    That seems it now.

## 'If You Had Known'

If you had known
When listening with her to the far-down moan
Of the white-selvaged and empurpled sea,
And rain came on that did not hinder talk,
Or damp your flashing facile gaiety
In turning home, despite the slow wet walk
By crooked ways, and over stiles of stone:
      If you had known

You would lay roses,
Fifty years thence, on her monument, that discloses
Its graying shape upon the luxuriant green;
Fifty years thence to an hour, by chance led there,
What might have moved you? – yea, had you foreseen
That on the tomb of the selfsame one, gone where
The dawn of every day is as the close is,
      You would lay roses!

## The Marble Tablet

There it stands, though alas, what a little of her
    Shows in its cold white look!
Not her glance, glide, or smile; not a tittle of her
    Voice like the purl of a brook;
      Not her thoughts, that you read like a book.

It may stand for her once in November
    When first she breathed, witless of all;
Or in heavy years she would remember
    When circumstance held her in thrall;
      Or at last, when she answered her call!

Nothing more. The still marble, date-graven,
    Gives all that it can, tersely lined;
That one has at length found the haven
    Which every one other will find;
      With silence on what shone behind.

## Days to Recollect

Do you recall
That day in Fall
When we walked towards Saint Alban's Head,
Over thistledown that summer had shed,
Or must I remind you?
Winged thistle-seeds which hitherto
Had lain as none were there, or few,
But rose at the brush of your petticoat-seam
(As ghosts might rise of the recent dead),
And sailed on the breeze in a nebulous stream
Like a comet's tail behind you:
You don't recall
That day in Fall?

Then do you remember
That sad November
When you left me never to see me more,
And looked quite other than theretofore,
As if it could not *be* you?
And lay by the window whence you had gazed
So many times when blamed or praised,
Morning or noon, through years and years,
Accepting the gifts that Fortune bore,

Sharing, enduring, joys, hopes, fears!
Well: I never more did see you. –
Say you remember
That sad November!